# How To Stop Being Insensitive

*Step By Step Blueprint On How To Stop Being An Insensitive Person, Be More Empathetic, Stop Hurting People, Stop Being Toxic, and More To Build Healthy Relationships*

D1519622

# Introduction

There comes a time when you look at your relationships and wonder how they got where they are. This is especially true when others accuse you of being toxic and insensitive despite your efforts to contribute to the relationship's well-being.

You may feel like giving up or lashing out. Or, you may demand some respect or become defensive as you try to state your views. Unfortunately, none of those things end up well for you. And while that can be frustrating, there is no need to give up. You only need to approach the issue differently, which is where this book comes in.

Follow through as we discuss what it means to be insensitive and the steps you can take to come out of that trap, leave toxicity behind and build healthy relationships.

Let's begin with the first step!

PS: I'd like your feedback. If you are happy with this book, please leave a review on Amazon.

Please leave a review for this book on Amazon by visiting the page below:

https://amzn.to/2VMR5qr

# Table of Content

**Introduction** _____ 2

**Chapter 1: Learn To Recognize Insensitive Behavior** _____ 6

**Chapter 2: Be Ware Of The Root Cause Of Insensitivity** _____ 22

The Root Cause of Insensitivity ___ 22

**Chapter 3: Improve Your Empathy** _____ 34

Empathy-building Strategies _____ 35

**Chapter 4: Use Empathetic Words And Actions** _____ 46

**Chapter 5: Build a Strong Relationship** _____ 57

# Chapter 6: Be More Understanding _____ 68

How to Become More Understanding _____ 70

# Chapter 7: Know What To Avoid 79

# Chapter 8: Work On Your Self-Awareness _____ 89

# Conclusion _____100

# Chapter 1: Learn To Recognize Insensitive Behavior

Many people fall into the trap of thinking that insensitivity is all about being tactless or saying and doing things that intentionally or unintentionally hurt other people. But that is only half of it. It also involves the things you don't say and do.

Imagine a scenario where the people in your life think you're insensitive but you're going on with your life without a clue. Then one day, perhaps during an argument, they list all the ways you've failed them.

What would you do? Of course, you'd sit there in shock, not believing the words coming from their mouths, and then you'll react, and what you say and do may make or break your relationship.

That's a chilling scenario. And perhaps you've already gone through it.

The next step is to delve deeper into what it means to be insensitive. Being insensitive has certain attitudes and behaviors. You are insensitive when you:

## *Speak the whole truth*

Words have power. They can heal or hurt depending on how we use them. And while you don't want to make a habit of lying to others, there are times when speaking the whole truth hurts more than heals.

To illustrate, let's take the example of a woman called Alice.

Alice and her husband Petro had three kids before the age of thirty and thought they had closed the chapter on having kids. But thirteen years later, Alice learned she was pregnant despite taking all precautions not to get pregnant. She gave birth to a baby girl who, unlike her siblings, was not planned.

The problem was that Alice let the kid know she 'came from an unwanted pregnancy.' Over the years, the kid grew up listening to that same rhetoric (often told like an old joke) and, as a result, started wishing she hadn't been born. In this case, Alice was insensitive and also incredibly mean to her child. That was one truth the child could have done without knowing.

### *Say hurtful things*

Some words bring nothing but hurt to others. These include words such as:

- 'Are you stupid?'

- 'Are you deaf?'

- 'Are you blind?'

- 'You can't get anything right!'

- 'You're fat.'

- 'You're ugly.'

- 'You should never have been born.'

- 'No one loves you.'

- 'You're worthless' and so forth

We usually use such words in a fit of anger, and their intention may be to point out a mistake made by the addressee. But instead of pointing to the person's behavior, they launch a personal attack on the individual. They are mean and degrading.

Additionally, some of these statements have a strain of ableism since they refer to physical disabilities. Using such words as an insult shows a high level of insensitivity.

## Tell offensive jokes

Offensive jokes can be funny, but they can also offend some people. Consider an example of a joke that refers to a famous Bible tale. It goes:

*"I can accept a virgin being pregnant but having three wise men in the same venue? Come on now! Who wrote that?"*

This joke may be funny when told to a group of women, but if there is a man in that group, it becomes insensitive simply because it implies that wise men are a rare species, and it is impossible to find more than two of them at a gathering.

Imagine if the joke came from a man with the words 'wise men' replaced with 'blondes' and told to a group of women. No one would be laughing. But some would laugh if the same were told to a group of men.

That is the nature of insensitive jokes. They can be harmless fun in certain contexts, but they hurt others and leave a bad impression about the speaker outside that context. In other words, that joke you think is harmless can make you look like an insensitive jerk.

## Fail to be observant

One of the things that can make you look insensitive is failing to be observant. When you don't notice the things going on with the people you interact with, you show you're not concerned with what's going on in their lives.

You must train yourself to observe the 'little things.' Some things may seem unimportant to you, but be very important to other people. For example, something like your partner's new hairstyle may seem small but signify the care and hard work that went into achieving it. When you notice it, you're essentially letting your partner know that you are invested in their life.

## *Fail to listen*

Listening is an active skill that requires you to:

- Listen attentively to the person

- Understand what they are saying and

- Respond appropriately

If someone is talking to you and you're busy watching television or texting on your phone instead of looking at them and paying attention to what they're saying, you'll show that you're not interested in listening to them.

Also, if you don't take the time to understand the meaning behind their words, actions, and body language, you will find it difficult to respond to their needs, which will paint you in a bad light. At the end of the day, how you respond to the things you've heard is the very thing that shows the value you place on them.

## Monopolize the conversation

When conversing with others, you must do your best not to monopolize the conversation. Remember, every person has their own thoughts, experiences, and ideas. When you monopolize the conversation, you deny them the chance to express themselves.

## Give unfiltered opinions

While it is true that everyone has the right to their own opinion, it is also true that your opinion can make you seem insensitive.

For instance, telling someone dealing with fertility issues that they can always adopt instead of trying for a baby is insensitive. That's a personal matter that is not any of your business. Unless asked, you must refrain from stating your opinion on such matters.

## *Fail to pick up on social cues*

Social cues are the unspoken or nonverbal part of interactions. They are important because they can tell you what someone is feeling. If you fail to pick up on them, you may end up inconveniencing people.

Some social cues you need to pick up on include:

- **Eye contact**: When talking to someone, you can tell if they are uncomfortable, engaged, or disengaged based on whether or not their eyes meet yours. For example, if someone is looking at their watch or looking at the door, they may have other engagements, and if you keep them there, you will be inconveniencing them.

- **Crossed arms**: Crossed arms could indicate that the person you're talking to is closed off, distressed, or uncomfortable. For instance, if you're lecturing someone and they cross their arms, they may be trying to protect themselves from the words you're saying. In this case, you need to check your tone and relax your stance to appear less threatening.

- **Posture**: You can tell whether someone is sad, excited, or tired by looking at their posture. For instance, you can tell when someone is tired if they are hunching their shoulders.

- **Proximity**: People tend to move closer to a speaker when they find the conversation engaging. For example, if someone leans towards you as you tell him a story, he is interested in what you're saying.

- **Facial expressions:** Someone's facial expressions can indicate boredom, agitation, and annoyance.

- **Fidgeting** – Some people tend to fidget when they feel uncomfortable or uninterested in the conversation.

You can learn to recognize and understand social cues by sharpening your observations. It is also just as important to learn about different cultures and individual tendencies before jumping to conclusions.

For instance, some people tend to fidget out of habit or due to social anxiety; other people avoid eye contact so as not to seem disrespectful. If you fail to recognize the meaning behind their actions, you may end up saying or doing things that hurt them.

## *Ask inappropriate questions*

Some questions seem harmless enough but may come off as insensitive based on the circumstances of the person being asked the question. Such questions include:

- Are you pregnant?

- What's your ethnicity?

- Have you lost weight?

- Are you a woman or a man?

- Where is her dad?

- When will you have children?

- Why are you single?

- Can't you afford that?

- Is that a scar? Where did you get it?

- Why is your car in the handicapped spot?

Such questions seek to extract certain information. However, that information may be extremely personal, or the person may not know you well enough or be comfortable enough to share the information. Thus, if you ask them such questions, you are putting them on the spot and coming off as insensitive.

### Confront others publicly

If you need to confront someone, you should do it privately and respectfully. Otherwise, you'll end up embarrassing the person. This is something you need to keep in mind, especially when dealing with kids. Parents or guardians may have no qualms about confronting their peers in private, but they don't extend that courtesy to their kids. Remember, kids have feelings too. Don't shame them in public.

## *Complain frequently*

Frequent complaints do little to change your circumstances especially when directed at someone who has no control over the situation. If you have a problem with someone or a certain situation, don't form a habit of telling everyone else about the problem. Instead, arrange to speak to the person, raise the issue, and be ready to listen to what the person has to say.

## *Minimize another's pain*

When someone tells you about some complexity in their life, do not try to minimize their pain. If you dismiss, deny or reject their words, you're telling them their experience is insignificant, unacceptable, or inaccurate. Do not use words such as:

- 'It could be worse.'

- 'At least it's not X or Y.'

- 'That's life.'

- 'It happened so long ago. Get over it!'

- 'You shouldn't think that way.'

- 'You shouldn't feel like that' or

- 'Just stop thinking about it.'

Such statements are cold and insensitive, and you should do your best to avoid them. Also, avoid rolling your eyes, waving your hand dismissively, or scoffing when someone tells you about their experience.

Additionally, please do not take that as an opportunity to tell the person other horrid stories that make their own experience seem inferior. All you need to do is listen and acknowledge their pain, even if you don't agree with their viewpoint.

As you can see, you may be doing some things that may be causing you to appear insensitive. The best thing to do is learn about them and avoid them. Another thing you can do is look at the root cause of insensitivity.

# Chapter 2: Be Ware Of The Root Cause Of Insensitivity

What is the root cause of insensitivity?

Well:

Surprisingly, insensitivity does not always come cloaked in a lack of concern for others. It can come from a place of caring, so it is prudent to look at yourself and determine what drives your insensitivity.

## The Root Cause of Insensitivity

The root cause of insensitivity includes:

### *Self-centeredness*

Self-centeredness is a common trait in insensitive people because they tend to focus on themselves more; they are often concerned with their interests and welfare, which makes it easier for them to ignore other people's needs.

Let's make it clear:

It is not a crime to look out for yourself. But even as you do so, you must observe the people in your vicinity and determine how your actions affect them. Let's illustrate using the example of Chris and Janine.

The two are married and have three kids below the age of twelve. They also work full-time jobs. As such, they need to cooperate to take care of the kids and the house chores.

If one of them comes home from work and decides they've had a long, hard day and don't want to do anything else, the other will have no choice but to deal with everything by themselves, which any tired person might find overwhelming.

Self-centeredness makes you see your pain and ignore the other person's pain. And once you do that, you end up hurting your loved ones.

## *A lack of empathy*

This point closely relates to the previous point. When you focus on yourself and your experiences, dismissing someone else's experiences and pain points becomes easier.

Empathy calls for you to put yourself in the other person's shoes so that you can understand their feelings, needs, and intentions. If you lack empathy, you won't feel bothered to understand what others are going through. Rather, you'll be quick to judge them harshly.

Let's take the example of a woman on the receiving end of several verbal and written attacks. The woman had placed a toddler on a mat and was busy chatting on her phone. A stranger snapped her photo and posted it on social media, saying how parents nowadays were more concerned with being online than looking after their kids, and the comments were vicious. Only later did people learn that the woman was at the airport and she and her kid had traveled for long hours.

The toddler was tired from the journey, and the woman placed the toddler on a mat to allow him to stretch as she called her partner to let them know they'd arrived safely and he should come to get them.

Funnily, people who took the time to study the photo deduced the situation because they understood how tiring it was for both mother and child to travel for long hours. They showed more empathy than the stranger who posted the photo for likes and those who were quick to post vile comments because they failed to put themselves in the woman's shoes.

## *Taking pride in speaking out*

Speaking up to call out an injustice or for yourself are admirable things that come from caring. However, when you do such things, your intention should never be to embarrass anyone.

Here's a story:

An elderly couple was taking a trip to visit their daughter one day when they decided to board a bus. The bus came to a stop, and a pregnant woman and a man entered, but there was nowhere to sit. The man noticed a young man and politely asked him if the pregnant woman could sit there, and the young man politely refused.

The elderly couple was not amused; they scolded the young man, saying how disrespectful young people are nowadays. It wasn't until the young man raised his shirt up to show his bandaged torso and explained that he was just from surgery and still feeling woozy that the couple kept quiet and then started apologizing for their hurtful comments. They'd spoken out without knowing the whole story, embarrassing the young man.

Before you speak up, gauge the situation and determine how best to go about it. This way, you won't end up causing more problems in your pursuit of justice.

## *Impulsivity*

Impulsivity is the act of reacting to things without much thought. When you engage in this toxic behavior, you may find yourself:

- Changing plans abruptly

- Canceling plans

- Destroying property

- Having frequent outbursts

- Jumping to conclusions and so forth

Now, take a minute to study the behaviors associated with impulsivity. Let's take the first one.

Let's say you made plans with your friends to meet somewhere for dinner, but you abruptly cancel the plans. It may seem like a little thing to you, but many people need to make certain arrangements to meet up with others. For instance, they may need to get out of work earlier, find a babysitter or even change their plans to accommodate you.

If you change your plans without giving them enough time to adjust their plans, it will show a high level of insensitivity on your part.

## *Immaturity*

Immaturity refers to how a grownup uses childish antics to deal with situations. When you are immature, you fail to consider other people's feelings, especially when they want to discuss certain topics. You may:

- Laugh if someone asks you to discuss various issues

- Pretend you have something else to do

- Postpone the discussion every time it comes up

- Say you're too stressed or too tired to talk now and

- Find excuses and blame other people and situations instead of taking responsibility

But you must understand that you can only delay having tough conversations for so long.

Things don't get better because you ignore them; they only get worse because ignoring tough conversations sends the message that you don't care enough to have them. That's the type of message that hurts other people's feelings and causes cracks in relationships.

## *Learning to be unbothered*

Insensitivity can be a learned trait. It happens when you grow up in a world where you must hide your emotions or fight to survive. As such, you close yourself up and expect other people to solve their own problems just like you solve your own.

If you grew up in an environment that made it feel like asking for help is a sign of weakness, you might fail to reach out to others because you don't know how. You need to unlearn this if you want to build healthy relationships.

Another thing you need to guard yourself against is being insensitive to people because of the labels you've assigned them.

We often label people based on things like:

- The amount of money they possess

- Ethnicity

- Gender

- Marital status

- Celebrity

- Political affiliations

- Educational background and

- Religion

You may notice that you often show a blatant lack of concern for people you consider better or worse off than you. For example, you may dismiss someone's pain because they are rich.

Or, you may make an insensitive comment when someone with a different political affiliation or marital status complains about their circumstances.

If you really want to stop being insensitive, you must learn to see people as individuals instead of as labels.

## *Avoidance*

Sometimes you may fail to reach out to other people because you think doing so would be a hassle. For instance, if you are an introvert and someone invites you to a social gathering, you may decide to put on headphones and sit in a corner instead of socializing with others because you don't want to be overwhelmed by the situation. However, your friends and family members who may have been waiting to see you may feel awful because you snubbed them.

Also, some people tend to act cold toward others because they don't know how to help them. For instance, you may say nothing when you discover a friend has lost a loved one. Or, you may decide to keep away when someone is admitted to the hospital because you reason there is nothing you can do for them.

But no matter how you feel, you need to remember that insensitivity has to do with the things you say and do. Those are things within your control. You can stop being insensitive by learning what to say and what to do in various situations. To do this, you need to brush up on your empathy-building strategies.

Let's see what this is about.

# Chapter 3: Improve Your Empathy

If you genuinely want to stop being insensitive, you must sharpen your empathy-building strategies.

Here's the thing:

Insensitivity is all about ignoring others, showing a lack of concern for them, being tactless when you talk to others, and doing and saying things that hurt them. On the other hand, empathy is about placing yourself in another person's shoes so you can understand their feelings, needs, and intentions.

Insensitivity hurts, but empathy causes you to pause, look at another person's viewpoint, and treat others with kindness and compassion. As such, if you focus on strategies that can help you build up your empathy,  you'll stop being insensitive, avoid engaging in toxic habits and build healthy relationships.

## Empathy-building Strategies

Some strategies you can use include:

### *Focus your attention outwards*

If you're not used to paying attention to people, you may not realize how insensitive you are unless someone points it out. But there is something you can do to teach yourself to focus outwards. You can start by paying attention to your surroundings.

As you know, there are certain things that you can do almost unconsciously because you're so used to doing them. For example, if you're used to driving to a certain place, you may arrive at your destination without remembering the things you saw on the journey. This is because the things you saw registered unconsciously.

So, unless something unexpected happens, it becomes easier to ignore other things.

Unfortunately, the same applies to the people you interact with. You may become so used to seeing them that you can't recall what they were wearing or doing when you spoke to them. That is the danger of familiarity. It makes you comfortable with putting things out of your mind, and when you do that, you breed insensitivity.

On the other hand, if you pay attention to the sights, smells, and sounds you encounter each day, you will learn to pay attention to the people in your life instead of taking them for granted.

## *Talk to others*

In life, we often have a lot of people around us. You have your family members, friends, colleagues, neighbors, and the people you meet as you go about your day. You can learn empathy by communicating with such people.

Think of someone you often talk to and ask yourself how much you know about that person. Do you know what they love to eat? The foods they hate? Their favorite color? Their dream destination? What they wanted to be when they were younger? What are their hobbies or favorite song?

These are things that can help you know the person better. Moreover, when someone talks about something they love or hate, they become more animated, and you'll discover the range of emotions they're capable of showing. Someone you thought of as boring or dull may become lively and animated when talking about their favorite hobby. And as you get to know them better, you'll learn to appreciate them.

## *Focus on listening*

As already stated, listening is an active skill. That means you can learn to cultivate good listening skills. For this exercise, you should train yourself to:

- **Be fully present when talking to others** - This means putting your phone down, shutting down your inner dialogue, and avoiding distractions while you converse with someone.

- **Listen to understand** – When you listen to understand, it means you have fully invested in what the person is saying instead of thinking about what to say. Listening to understand also calls on you to get the whole story instead of being too quick to react.

- **Practice good eye contact** – If someone is talking to you, you should turn to face them and maintain eye contact. This will let them know that you are fully present and invested in the conversation.

- **Notice non-verbal clues** – Make it a habit to notice non-verbal clues. Look at the person's posture, facial expressions, proximity, and tone of voice. These things will help you understand what they are not saying out loud.

- **Ask questions** – You should practice asking open-ended questions that can help you understand the people you interact with in different aspects of your life. Open-ended questions help people up because they don't require a 'yes' or 'no' answer.

- **Paraphrase** – It is good to paraphrase what someone says to ensure you've gotten all the facts right.

- **Withhold judgment** – When conversing with someone, don't be too quick to pass judgment, give advice, or tell them about your own experience. Let the person speak, ask for clarification, and try to understand their feelings. If you make it easier for the person to open up, they may decide to ask you for advice. If they do, try to brainstorm different ideas and look at the situation from various perspectives instead of being judgmental. That will help the person arrive at a solution that is beneficial to him.

Remember that engaging in such exercises is about sharpening your listening skills and learning to treat others better. As such, you can act on one aspect of the skill and gradually strive to include the other aspects.

For instance, you can focus on letting the other person finish what they have to say before speaking. Or, you can practicc paraphrasing what the person has said to ensure you are on the same page. As you add more skills, you will become better at listening to others and responding to their needs.

## *Challenge your prejudices*

What do you think of when you hear words such as homeless, gangster, terrorist, celebrity, blue check, YouTuber, baby daddy, and immigrant? We often associate such words with certain connotations, and those connotations affect the way we see people associated with such words. But if you look beyond your prejudices, you will discover that there are real people behind those words.

Let's take the example of a woman named Angie. Angie is homeless. She and her two kids live in her car. Many people don't know that Angie's family fell into hard times when her husband fell chronically ill. Angie had to take care of him, all while handling the family's expenses until he passed away. By then, they had depleted their resources, and Angie could no longer afford the rent. She and her kids started living in her car to survive.

But despite all that, people who don't know her frown at her and hurl abuses at her when they learn she is homeless because they associate homelessness with drugs and laziness. It never occurs to them that she is working to pay off the debts and to keep her kids healthy and in school.

What's the lesson here?

The lesson here is that you need to check your prejudices and refrain from judging others. If you can't say or do something helpful, live and let live.

## *Prepare to take action*

As much as you'd love to change your ways, it would be wise to prepare yourself before you take action. As we've seen, there are various root causes of insensitivity. You must be prepared to confront your thinking if you are genuinely committed to eliminating toxic traits that make you seem insensitive.

This is why you should:

### **Know your motivation**

It's important to keep your goal in sight when you're trying to shed off insensitive behavior.

This will help you work hard to achieve what you want. Do you want to build a better relationship with your family? Do you want to communicate better? Do you wish to know other people better? Such goals are commendable but only achievable through action. But if you keep them in mind, you'll find the motivation to make meaningful changes.

## Be courageous

You will need some courage if you wish to stop being insensitive. That is because you may need to deal with people you've ignored for months or even years. Some of them may have grown used to you ignoring them and may be suspicious when you start treating them differently; your behavior may have hurt others. So, take steps to reach out to them and be prepared for their reaction.

## Be prepared to put in the work

You must put in the work if you wish to see changes. You must change how you think and how you see other people. You must learn to talk and act in ways that will not cause harm to others. Strive for excellence instead of striving for perfection. This way, you'll be conscientious of your actions and strive to do better even when some things don't go your way.

After all, it is by taking action that you can change your circumstances and build healthier relationships. To that end, let's look at some words and actions you can use in your day-to-day life to show that you care about the people in your life.

# Chapter 4: Use Empathetic Words And Actions

The only way to stop being insensitive and get rid of toxic behavior is to develop good habits that show you care about others. You can do this by using empathetic words and actions.

When you interact with others, you need to:

### *Acknowledge their pain*

When someone is hurting, they want to know they are not alone. Even if you don't have the means to help them, they will feel supported if you show them you are trying to understand what they are going through.

Some words you can use include:

- 'I'm sorry that happened to you:

- 'That sucks!'

- 'I hate that this happened.'

- 'That must be hard.'

- 'That sounds challenging.'

Remember, words are powerful. They can validate someone else's feelings. So, learn to speak up instead of avoiding the person or subject because you feel powerless.

## *Share your feelings*

Other people cannot read your mind. If they tell you something or if you notice that they are going through something, you need to let them know how you feel. This way, they will see that you're not unaffected.

You can say something like:

- 'I have no idea what to say:

- 'I can't imagine what you're going through.'

- 'My heart hurts for you.'

- 'That makes me really sad.'

- 'I wish I could do something to make it better.'

Don't hide your feelings or try to be strong in the face of difficulties. The emotions you show will let others know that you are in this together and that you can work together to forge ahead despite your circumstances.

### *Show interest*

It only takes a few minutes to show someone you are interested in what they are saying or going through. Apart from giving them your full attention, it would be best to ask questions that show your interest in the conversation.

You can use words such as:

- 'How are you feeling about that?'

- 'What's that been like for you?'

- 'Are you serious? And then what happened?'

Remember, many people find comfort in talking about their circumstances. The time you take to listen to someone may mean a lot to them.

## *Encourage them*

We may sometimes fail to empathize with others because we hold them in high regard. As such, we assume they are on top of their game and things will work out for them. But it is good to note that everyone could use encouraging words now and then.

Some words you can use include:

- 'You are brave.'

- 'That was smart.'

- 'I'm proud of you.'

- 'You're a warrior.'

- 'You matter.'

- 'I love you.'

- 'Your dreams are valid.'

- 'I'm with you.'

- 'I'm in your corner.'

Apart from saying the words, you can take the time to write them on a card. This will show the person you really put some thought into what you're saying.

As an individual, remember that your experiences and upbringing impact your words and actions. As such, you may be too quick to put another person down if they tell you something you perceive to be beyond their reach. For example, if someone tells you they want to be a musician and you laugh at them or tell them to forget it, it may crush the person.

On the other hand, you can ask them questions about what type of music they want to make, what musicians they listen to, or which platforms they would like to showcase their music on. By listening to them and encouraging them to speak, you may help them rcalize the steps they need to take to make their dreams come true.

## *Thank them for opening up*

It's not easy for some people to open up. They may have mentally gone over the scenario for a while before they got the courage to speak to you. You can show them that you appreciate the effort and struggle they went through to speak to you

You can use words such as:

- 'Thank you for sharing that.'

- 'I'm glad you talked about it's

- 'Thank you for telling me. That means a lot.'

- 'Thanks for opening up to me.'

And remember, when someone opens up to you, it shows a level of trust. As such, you must be careful to guard that trust. Don't gossip about the person. If you wish to reach out to someone else you think can help, discuss it with the person first.

### *Support them*

Empathy should not stop at kind words. You can take it a step further and offer your support. Think about it. Let's say a friend tells you they haven't eaten in a significant while. If you have food in your house but instead of offering to give them some, you verbally sympathize with them, you will come off as insensitive because you failed to discern that your friend needs more than words in this instance.

Some words and actions you can use to show support to someone include:

- 'How can I help?'

- 'What do you need right now?'

- 'I'm here for you.'

- 'I'm here whenever you want to talk.'

Apart from using supportive words, you can show your support to others by doing several things. These include:

- **Give them a hug** – Sometimes, people need some external comfort. A hug can do so.

- **Buy a thoughtful gift** – To buy a thoughtful gift, you need to learn what someone likes or dislikes and what they need to make their life a little bit easier.

- **Volunteer your time** – If you can, you should seriously consider volunteering your time.

- **Stop to help someone in need** – Open the door for someone, help them find something they need, or take time to answer their question.

- **Get practical** – If someone tells you they want to exercise to improve their health, you can offer to join them from time to time.

- **Teach someone a skill** – Think of a skill you can teach someone and do so. You can teach skills such as budgeting, time management, or cooking. Such skills would go a long way to make someone's life easier.

- **Offer to babysit** – Babysitting is something you can do to give parents or guardians a break and allow them to rejuvenate.

- **Buy food for someone** – If someone is having a hard time, you can buy them some food or cook for them.

- **Do some chores for someone in need** – Look around and see what needs to be done and offer your help.

- **Create a care package** – A care package can include books, soup dishes, tea, chocolate, and other things.

As mentioned, the things you do or don't do determine whether you're insensitive. If your intentions are good, but your words and actions end up hurting others, you need to reevaluate your thinking and actions. That's just how it is and what you need to do. It isn't just about you.

Rather, it is about you, the people in your life, and how you interact with them.

If you want others to view your words and actions in a positive life, they must impact them positively. A great way to get to the point where you openly show you care about the people in your life is by building a strong relationship with them.

Let's see how you can do that.

# Chapter 5: Build a Strong Relationship

There is no trick to building strong relationships. You only need to do little, everyday things that help you cement your relationship with others.

The little things you do are powerful enough to turn a stranger into an acquaintance, turn an acquaintance into a friend, and even turn a friend into a close friend. And as you get to know the other person, you'll know their likes and dislikes, which will greatly decrease the chances of you unknowingly hurting them with your words and deeds.

So, what can you do to build strong relationships? You can:

## *Show your appreciation*

Think back to the time you did something for someone, and they were really appreciative. How did that make you feel? Now, think of the time you went out of your way to do something nice, and the person barely acknowledged your presence. What did you think?

Obviously, as humans, we are impacted by the actions of others. Thus, it is not unusual to gravitate toward people who appreciate your efforts. The same is true of others. People like it when you acknowledge their efforts. They appreciate it when you tell them 'thank you' and praise them for their actions.

But there's something else you need to know.

You leave room for your friendship to grow when you show your appreciation. To illustrate, let's say a colleague you've never spoken to holds the door for you because they see you carrying a lot of stuff. If you walk away without saying a word, you'll remain distant. But if you say thank you, that colleague will find it easier to greet you the next time you meet.

It's the little things you do that build a relationship.

Unfortunately, people tend to forget to do the little things after they've known each other for a while. As such, they learn to take the people in their life for granted; before long, their actions start hurting others. This should not be the case. Little things matter.

Words like sorry, excuse me, forgive me, and thank you are powerful words that should not be left unspoken, no matter how long you've known someone else.

## *Open the lines of communication*

When you fail to communicate with the people in your life, you will start losing touch with them because people do not remain stagnant. They grow. Their feelings about things change, their taste changes, and they find other interests.

Those are things you fail to notice when you distance yourself from them. And we're not just talking about physical distance here. We're also talking about emotional distance.

If you fail to communicate with your loved ones, you'll create a wedge between you; this wedge will make it easier to ignore the things right in front of you.

Here are some key things you can do to ensure that does not happen:

- **Check-in with your loved ones** – This world is full of uncertainties. You need to check in with your loved ones to let them know you're safe and thinking about them. For example, if you visited a loved one and then returned to your place, you can send them a message letting them know you arrived safely. It seems like a small thing to do, but doing so will positively affect your relationship.

- **Make communication a habit** – Technology has made it easier to communicate with others. Don't wait until you have something important to say to communicate with your loved ones. Instead, make it a habit to call them, chat with them and send them jokes and gif videos as you go about your day. If you spend hours chatting with strangers, you can spare a few minutes to chat with your friends and family.

- **Solve problems as a team** – The people in your life are part of your team. As such, whenever a problem arises, you should come together to brainstorm ways to solve it. If you make big decisions on your own without consulting your team members, you'll essentially be letting them know you don't value their input.

- **Make time to evaluate your relationships** – It is good to evaluate personal relationships from time to time. This will help you see how you've been treating the people in your life. For instance, you can go through your phone contacts and ask yourself when you last had an in-depth conversation with the people in your contact list. You have some work to do if you can't remember or if it was long ago.

Remember, there is a difference between seeing someone each day and actually taking the time to have a meaningful conversation with them. Don't let familiarity make you believe you can get away with doing the bare minimum. Communication is a gift. Use it to build a strong relationship with your loved ones.

## Invest in trustworthiness

Lies have the power to destroy a relationship. They are like daggers that stab the heart and leave wounds and scars long after they've been told. But while many people avoid telling outright lies, some are too comfortable with telling little lies and not keeping their word.

Let's take the example of a guy called Albert. Albert has three siblings and is the second born. He and his siblings all live in their own places, but they usually meet up at their parent's or sibling's house every other month. However, Albert would have an excuse when it came to meeting at his house, often saying it was just easier to meet up at his sibling's place since it was larger. And when it came to family gatherings, he always forgot to bring something someone had told him to bring.

Everyone took it in good stride, and Albert didn't think much about it until he found out he was the only one in his family who had no important part in his brother's wedding. The same thing happened during other special family occasions. Though they loved him, his family could not trust him to do what was expected when it was expected; thus, they left him out of the planning.

That's what untrustworthiness does. It makes people doubt your commitment and question whether or not you care for them. And if worse comes to worst, the people in your life will simply write you off as insensitive and stop relying on you. That type of damage takes a lot of work to repair. And the only way to do so is by showing that you are trustworthy with the little things. Show up when you're meant to show up. Do what you said you'd do and become a pillar of support to the people in your life. That's how to build a strong relationship.

## *Spend time together*

Your time is one of the most important things in this world. You need to value it highly and spend it wisely.

Think back to the number of hours you spent in school. How many friends did you make, and how many are still your friends today?

We have grown conditioned to the belief that the friendships we make in school are fleeting and to think of the people we spend hours working next to as work colleagues or friends.

Thus, instead of forming strong friendships with such people, they form shallow friendships based on the things they have in common, and anyone who has different interests is seen as an outsider. That is not how friendship should work.

Friendship should be about finding out each other's likes and dislikes, acknowledging different viewpoints, respecting other people's choices, and accommodating each other whenever possible. If you view friendship like this, you will develop a genuine interest in other people.

Instead of being cold and unconcerned about their lives, you will inquire about them simply because you've come to understand that such things are important to that person, and you don't need to have everything in common to show that you are about others. Rather, you care because you want them in your circle. They are your team, and just like a soccer team, not all members can be strikers or goalkeepers, but the whole team can become stronger by understanding each other and learning to play as a team.

Never forget the people in your circle and your team. As such, you need to look out for each other, work to get better together, and brainstorm together whenever problems crop up. If you do that, you'll grow stronger together and build the type of team anyone would be proud to belong to.

But even as you arrive to build a stronger team, you should not forget to be more understanding. This is because being understanding will impact you greatly.

Let's see what this is about.

# Chapter 6: Be More Understanding

Now that you know that the people in your life are your team, there is something else you need to know. You need to be more understanding if you wish to build up the people in your life instead of tearing them down and hurting their feelings.

Remember, a team only works best when its members work together. But if you devalue other members and ignore their contributions to the team, you will exhibit toxic behavior that will wreak havoc on your relationships. Such behavior includes:

- Blaming others

- Being overly critical

- Being judgmental

- Spreading negativity

- Engaging in rude behavior

- Exuding rigidness instead of being flexible

- Exhibiting recklessness in your decision making

- Being quick to anger

- Being arrogant

- Being stingy

- Being apathetic and

- Embracing absolutism and seeing things as black or white

Such toxic behavior sends the message that you are only concerned with your interests and do not care enough about the other person to pause and think before you react. Fortunately, being more understanding will help you avoid toxicity.

# How to Become More Understanding

To be more understanding, you should:

### *Recognize other perspectives*

When you put yourself in someone else's shoes, you understand where they are coming from and what led to their decisions. This enables you to be more understanding towards them even if you don't share the same perspective. However, it would be hard for you to empathize with them if you can't figure out that they have a different point of view from yours. That is why you need to teach yourself to recognize when someone has differing views.

To do this, you should:

### *Learn from watching TV*

You can learn a lot about how people view things from watching television shows and movies. Soap operas, dramas, and crime shows are especially good at showing how different people view the same situation.

As you watch such shows, ask yourself what the characters are dealing with and what drove them to their decisions. For example, a character may take a bat to someone's car in an angry fit. Then as you get his back story, you may learn that the man is angry because the owner of the car made a false claim against him, costing him his job.

As the story proceeds, you may learn that the owner of the car felt like he had to pin his mistakes on someone else because he was afraid of getting fired over a mistake he'd made since he had a wife and kids depending on him and getting fired would put him in a difficult position.

Now, of course, you'll have your own opinions of what the characters did, and may you find yourself approving or disapproving of their actions even as you learn what drove them to it. But the fact that you took time to see things from their perspective will impact how you react to them. Thus, your reactions will have a tinge of sympathy, and you may seek solutions to their various problems instead of completely writing them off.

## *Use your imagination*

You can use your imagination to picture different scenarios and how you would react to them, given different circumstances. The purpose of this exercise is to show you that there is no one way to react to something. If you learn that, you will be less likely to react rudely to something others say or do because you don't agree with them.

Also, when you go through different scenarios, you'll be more conscious of how you treat others since you realize that some behaviors border on insensitivity.

## *Learn from your own experiences*

In life, you go through various experiences. Such experiences can help you look at things from various perspectives. For example, think of a time you were unfairly punished for doing something. If you recall the feelings you had at that time, you will teach yourself to do your research before you jump to conclusions when dealing with other people.

If you spend time thinking of how people have treated you throughout the years and how you wish to be treated, you'll learn to recognize when others expect more from you. To illustrate, let's say you had a good experience at a social gathering because someone reached out to you and introduced you to other people. You can use that experience to make other people feel welcome whenever you attend social gatherings.

You can learn from both negative and positive experiences.

If someone hurt you deeply due to how they behaved, ask yourself what they did that made you feel and avoid doing the same to others. This will show that you understand the power that words and actions have and you are willing to break the cycle of toxic behavior.

### *Give validation*

A great way to show that you understand what someone is going through is by acknowledging their thoughts, experiences, beliefs, values, and emotions. Validating someone does not mean that you like or agree with what he is saying. Rather, it shows you are present and care enough about them to listen to their hopes, dreams, and worries.

You give validation if you:

- **Give verbal responses** – If someone is talking to you, you can use verbal responses to show you're listening. You can use words such as 'I see,' 'okay,' and 'uh-huh' as the person talks to encourage him to go on.

- **Use your body language** – Your body language needs to let the other person know you're listening. Turn towards them, look them in their eyes, and nod where necessary.

- **Remain present** – Sometimes, you can use gestures to show you are present. For example, if someone tells you a painful story, you can pay them on their shoulder to offer them some comfort.

- **Ask questions** – Questions help move the conversation forward. When you ask someone questions relating to what they are saying, they will be encouraged to open up more, which will help them heal and release their tension.

- **Quiet your urge to criticize others** – Try not to criticize the person as he opens up to you. There is no need to tell him what you would have done in the same situation and make it seem like he was weak for reacting the way he did. Also, please don't belittle their feelings by telling them to get over what has happened. Instead, listen to them and empathize with them.

As you validate someone, they may ask you questions about what you would have done. If they do, you can let them know how you would approach the situation or advise them on what to do. But even as you do so, try to work with the person to find suitable solutions.

## Stop keeping score

Relationships have ups and downs.

If you focus on keeping score every time someone in your life does something that disappoints you, it may make you react coldly toward the person whenever you perceive that they haven't done what you want.

For example, if you ask your partner to take out the trash and he didn't do it, and you note that down, the next time you come home, and it's his time to cook, you may fly into a fit of rage Instead of giving him time to explain if you find that he hasn't done so. But if you'd stopped to ask, he may tell you that he'd ordered takeout since he had a bad day and didn't feel like cooking.

When you keep score, you use past mistakes to judge present mistakes, leading to more misunderstandings and arguments. That is why it is important to learn to forgive others and be more understanding toward them.

If you do that, you'll look at each problem as it arises instead of lumping past mistakes with present ones, which will help you build a stronger relationship.

Now that you know what to do to stop being insensitive, let's look at some things you need to avoid.

# Chapter 7: Know What To Avoid

You should endeavor to avoid certain things if you wish to build stronger relationships with others. Remember, we've said it again and again. Your words and actions have power. They could make you seem insensitive even if you weren't trying to be so. That is why you should strive to make changes.

You should do your best to avoid things like:

## *Mental health language*

Some people are really comfortable with using mental health language to describe their everyday situations. You'll find them using words such as PTSD, OCD, Bipolar, and ADD when describing everyday behaviors. For example, someone may say, 'I'm so bipolar about drinking soda with hamburgers,' to explain that he sometimes feels like he would rather not drink soda when eating a hamburger.

Or, another person may say, 'I'm OCD about keeping my desk clean.' Such statements underplay the impact of real mental health disorders, and you should not use them lightly.

## *Non-inclusive language*

Inclusive language reflects someone's style and personal preference. For instance, some people would like it if you refer to them using gendered pronouns such as 'She' and 'He,' while others would like you to use gender-neutral pronouns such as 'Ze' and 'They' when referring to them.

If you're unsure of the pronouns to use when talking to someone, you should ask them directly. Also, if someone tells you which pronouns they prefer, remember them and habitually use them whenever you talk to the person or about them.

## *Ageism*

Ageism involves stereotyping or discriminating against others due to their age. The practice is insensitive because it makes others feel as if they are not useful to society once they reach a certain age. For instance, if you have older people in your family, you may fail to include them in certain events because you think they are too old. Worse still, you may fail to seek their advice on various things simply because you think their thinking is outdated.

But ageism goes deeper than that. It affects how you see others and how you treat them. For example, if you see an older person working at Mcdonald's, you may ask him why he is doing the work of teenagers. Such comments hurt. That person is working hard to provide for himself and maybe others. Making it seem like the work is beneath him may come off as belittling his efforts.

While you may want the best for others, you must refrain from telling them that they should be earning more or have a higher position due to their age. Such well-meaning statements only make others feel that what they do is not enough.

Also, it is important to refrain from looking down on others due to their age. For instance, if you go to a hospital and find a young doctor, you shouldn't start questioning his qualifications and demanding a more qualified doctor. Instead, learn to respect people of all ages.

## *Microaggression*

Microaggression has to do with saying certain comments or doing certain things that are prejudicial towards marginalized individuals or groups. For example, if you've invited a POC to state his views on an important issue, you may comment by saying something like, 'You are so articulate.' By telling that person that, the unspoken part of your statement shows you do not expect POCs to be articulate, hence your surprise.

Telling a person of color that they are articulate is not a compliment. Rather, it exposes your prejudice.

If you are interested in praising the person, focus on the message, thought, or idea put forth rather than focusing on how he speaks. You can say something like, 'I like that idea,' and then proceed to say what exactly about it you like. This will show the person that you were listening to his ideas and are interested in what he has to say.

## Stereotypes

It's not good to have certain thoughts about a person due to gender, ethnicity, race, or religion. Humans are not monolithic. Thus, if you expect everyone belonging to a certain group to act the same way, you are not being fair.

Let's take the example of political affiliations.

If you expect someone to vote in a certain way due to their race or their gender, you are essentially telling them that their personal opinion doesn't matter. Everyone has the right to look at various political parties and determine which one they like best without being made to feel as if they are betraying their race or gender.

Stereotypes are harmful. They make you focus on a group as a whole instead of seeing the individual. Let's take the example of an Asian student struggling with his school work. His teacher assumed that all Asians are studious; thus, it took him a long time to figure out that the student needed extra help due to a learning disability. The teacher would focus on calling out the student and shaming him for being a bad Asian instead of trying to find out why the student was struggling.

Don't assume that people have certain capabilities or flaws due to stereotypes. Instead, learn to see people as individuals and treat them accordingly.

## *Tokenism*

Tokenism refers to how certain people, groups, or companies include people from a certain group in the hopes of appearing inclusive. For instance, if you have a company with a diversity issue and a POC employee, you may put him at the forefront of your diversity reforms.

You may expect the person to attend all the meetings about diversity, educate others on the issues facing marginalized individuals, and speak for everyone in his group. That places an enormous burden on the employee.

It would be good to remember that marginalized people still have individual thoughts, wants, and needs. They should not carry the emotional burden of a whole group. Plus, it should not be up to them to educate people who can easily read books or research various issues.

## *Tone policing*

Tone policing is something you need to avoid at all costs because it is incredibly rude and insensitive and seeks to put others down and belittle their message just because they put some emotion in their voice.

To illustrate, let's say that someone is upset with you and comes to you to talk about what is upsetting them. If you focus on their tone of voice and tell them to 'calm down' instead of focusing on what they are telling you, you are essentially telling them that their message does not mean much because they are 'too emotional.' As such, you fail to comprehend the issues the person has brought up because you are too busy pointing fingers at them. This works to destroy your relationship.

Always remember that others are entitled to their own emotions. When someone is sad or angry, it would be better to acknowledge their anger and ask how you can help improve things. This way, the person will understand that you are willing to hear them out, and they'll work with you to repair the damaged relationship.

Of course, changing how you speak or act may take time if you're used to being insensitive. But if you work on it consistently, there will come a time when such words and behavior will cease being part of you. This will go a long way to building your relationship with others.

As you work on that, you may also want to work on your self-awareness to achieve greater success in eliminating toxic words and actions.

Let's see what this is about.

# Chapter 8: Work On Your Self-Awareness

Self-awareness is something that can stop you in your tracks when you want to say or do things that hurt other people. That is because it has to do with understanding your thoughts and emotions. When you are self-aware, you'll understand the thoughts and emotions that drive your actions and recognize such thoughts and emotions in others.

For instance, let's say you have the habit of banging on the door whenever you argue with someone. If you reflect on your actions, you may determine that your actions stem from feeling misunderstood.

As such, if you see someone doing the same action, you may stop to think about what is driving their action and figure out another way to deal with them because you see yourself in them.

There are certain things you can do to work on your self-awareness. You need to:

### *Find out more about yourself*

Most people are too busy living to find out what they actually want in life.

Unfortunately, if you live without a purpose, you will find yourself doing things you don't like, which will surely negatively impact your words and actions.

That is why you must take the time to find out more about yourself.

- ✓ What are your values?

- ✓ What do you like?

- ✓ What do you dislike?

- ✓ What do you hope to achieve?

✓ What is your purpose?

If you find the answers to these questions, you will find it easier to express your wants and needs. This will make it easier for the people in your life to respond to your needs positively.

To illustrate, let's say you failed to get the job you wanted, and you let your loved one know. If you're looking for comfort and your loved one proceeds to lecture you on everything you should have done differently to increase your chances of getting the job, you will feel discouraged. In this case, you should know yourself well enough to tell your loved one what you need from them.

There is another advantage that comes with knowing more about yourself. This has to do with the people you attract in your life.

The more you know about yourself and what you want to achieve, the easier it shall be to find people with similar goals. For example, if you love to hike, you won't spend hours hanging out with people who love to sit at home and watch television. Rather, you'll look for friends who love to hike. This way, you and your friends will already have something in common before you begin building your relationship.

Of course, you wouldn't want to hang out only with people with the same interests as you. However, self-awareness will make it easier to hang out with people with other interests. For instance, if you are an introvert and have a friend who loves to party, self-awareness will help you find a suitable compromise.

In this example, you may decide to attend the party for a few minutes and then find a quiet place to sit. Alternatively, you may stick around for a bit and then head home early. This way, you can both enjoy each other's company without making the other feel overwhelmed.

## *Learn to be vulnerable*

When you open up to others, you invite them into your world and make it easier for them to invite you into theirs. This can help you build stronger relationships because it means everyone in the relationship is aware of the other person's wants, needs, hopes, and fears.

This knowledge helps the people in the relationship support each other and cheer for each other. There are various ways you can show vulnerability in a relationship. You need to:

## *Ask for what you need*

The first thing you can do is ask for what you need. If you need a hug, ask for it. If you wish for the people in your family to put away their phones when you sit down for a meal, ask them to do so. If you don't ask, you'll assume the other person cannot provide what you need, which will only pull you further apart.

Also, it would be wise to remember that others can't read your mind. You may be there fuming because they haven't done what you want when they have no idea of what you want in the first place.

### *Express what you think*

When you have a relationship with someone, the relationship is supposed to benefit both of you. That is why you need to express your thoughts and emotions truthfully.

If you hide your emotions and tell the other person what you assume he wants to hear, you will be doing him a disservice because only by being open can we learn from each other and grow stronger together.

## *Apologize for a mistake*

It's not easy to admit to making a mistake if you're not used to doing so. However, when you acknowledge your mistake and apologize for it, you're letting others know you are committed to making amends. But words are not enough when it comes to apologizing for your wrongdoings. You must also strive to change your behavior and avoid repeating the same mistakes.

All in all, you must remember that vulnerability is not a weakness. Rather, it lets you and your loved ones form stronger bonds as you get to know each other better. Thus, take the time to learn about your strengths and weakness and be open to sharing your thoughts with your loved ones.

## *Give it your best*

As an individual, you need to be aware of what you're doing and the effort you're putting into it. Doing this will help you build stronger relationships with the people in your life.

Think about it:

If you have issues in your relationship but do nothing or little to solve them, you will only end up causing more damage. But if you put 100 percent into the relationship and your partner does the same, you will be in a better position to repair and strengthen the relationship.

You can do various things to give your best to your relationship. You can:

- **Focus on the things you're doing** – When you're in a relationship, there will be instances where you find yourself doing things you don't like doing to make life easier for other people. For instance, you may cook because it is your turn to cook. If you put some effort into what you're doing, you will learn to make great meals that everyone will love and find enjoyable. But if you do the bare minimum, the people in your life will begin to think you don't value them enough to put in the effort.

- **Treat your appointments as important** – You must prioritize the people in your life. For example, if you decide to eat dinner together as a family, show up to dinner instead of making excuses for being late. Don't forget important dates, and don't go back on your promises. If you cannot make an appointment, say so beforehand and make alternative arrangements instead of casually dismissing the issue. As you know, your time is precious. As such, you should use it wisely and spend it making memories with the people you care about.

- **Take the initiative** – If you see something wrong or a friend or family member needs help, you need to take the initiative and offer your help. Some people find it hard to approach others when having a hard time. When you offer your help, they'll understand that you're there for them, and you're aware of what goes on in their lives. Also, it would be good to note when things are not going well for you. This way, you can tell someone about what you're going through and get the help and support you need to heal before you turn to bad habits.

- **Be part of the solution** -Self-awareness requires brutal honesty. Sometimes you'll learn that you're the one in the wrong and need to change your ways. For instance, being accused of being insensitive can wreak havoc on your emotions. But you can also choose to work on improving your relationship with others instead of being defensive. This may take work. It may take time, but showing you're willing to change will improve your relationship with others.

Fundamentally, you want to improve your self-awareness to avoid doing and saying things that harm you and others. But it is not enough to know how you think and feel. You should also look into how the things you do affect others. This way, you'll be able to stop toxic behavior before it even begins.

As your self-awareness increases, you will find it easier to build nourishing and peaceful relationships.

# Conclusion

While it is not realistic to expect perfection when it comes to how you treat other people, there is a lot you can do to avoid being insensitive. It starts with you being aware of your words and actions and how they affect the people you interact with. That will allow you to pause, take a closer look at the situation and see things from different perspectives.

When you do that, you'll be in a better position to show empathy to others and build healthy relationships.

PS: I'd like your feedback. If you are happy with this book, please leave a review on Amazon.

Please leave a review for this book on Amazon by visiting the page below:

https://amzn.to/2VMR5qr

Made in United States
Orlando, FL
07 June 2023

33898868R00055